L I F E  C L A S S : The Academic Male Nude 1820-1920

First published 1989 by GMP Publishers Ltd
 P O Box 247, London N17 9QR, England
This printed collection World Copyright © 1989 GMP Publishers Ltd
Individual drawings and paintings World Copyright © 1989 with the owners or St
Jude's Gallery
Introduction World Copyright © 1989 Edward Lucie-Smith
Caption texts World Copyright © 1989 Stephen Boyd
Designed and packaged 1989 by GMP Publishers Ltd
 P O Box 247, London N17 9QR, England
 telephone 01 365 1545 fax  01 365 1252

Distributed in North America by Alyson Publications Inc
 40 Plympton Street, Boston, MA 02118, USA

The drawings and paintings in this collection have all been exhibited by St
Jude's Gallery at one of their annual exhibitions of the Male Nude.
All enquiries should be addressed to:
St Jude's Gallery
107 Kensington Church Street, London W8, England
 telephone  01 727 8737

**British Library Cataloguing in Publication Data**

Life class: the academic male nude, 1820-1920
 1. Drawings. Special subjects. Men. Nudes, 1820-1920
 I. Boyd, Stephen
 743'.923'09034

 ISBN 0-85449-103-1

Printed and bound by Gilead Graphic Arts Ltd, Hongkong.

# LIFE CLASS

## *THE ACADEMIC MALE NUDE*
## 1 8 2 0 - 1 9 2 0

**Edited by Stephen Boyd**
**Introduced by Edward Lucie-Smith**

THE GAY MEN PRESS

The first great age of drawing and painting from the life began in the studios of the great Italian High Renaissance artists like Raphael, and reached a climax in the Academy founded in Bologna at the end of the 16th century by the brothers Annibale and Agostino Carracci and their cousin Lodovico. Throughout the 17th and 18th centuries artists continued to draw and paint from the life, using chiefly the nude male model. The models were male because painting was largely a man's profession. Female artists, such as Artemisia Gentileschi (1597-1651), now a feminist heroine, were very rare; they usually became painters through some kind of family connection. Artemesia was the daughter of Orazio Gentileschi (1562-1647), a well-regarded follower of Caravaggio. She was doubly an exception because she produced ambitious figurative work, whereas most successful women artists, such as Louise Moillon (1609/10-1696), who was French, and Maria Sibylla Merian (1647-1717), who was German, were confined to still life, or to natural history painting.

Attributed to
**Annibale Carracci** 1560-1609
Male Academic Drawing
red chalk
(42 x 28)cm

5

During the 18th century painting continued to be largely a masculine preserve, and the academic training codified by the Carracci continued to be the professional norm. Artists continued to be interested in drawing the male nude, even when the current of taste was turning towards a lighter and more feminine style of painting. G B Piazetta (1682-1754), for example, for a while ran a very successful life-class in Venice, and a number of drawings of the male nude by him and his pupils are known. But the femininity of the Rococo brought with it a fascination with the female body, and we can see this not only in the large numbers of drawings and paintings of the female nude produced by Franççois Boucher (1703-1770), the most prominent artist during the first half of the 18th century in France, but in the chubby, feminised type he often used when depicting males.

Attributed to
**Louis Gauffier** 1761-1801
Male Academic Drawing
black & white chalks

Boucher was closely associated with the French court, who supplied him with the greater part of his patronage. He enjoyed the particular favour of Mme de Pompadour. He was opposed on both political and aesthetic grounds by Jacques-Louis David (1748-1825), his successor as the dominant force in French art. David's major paintings – *The Oath of the Horatii* (1785), *The Death of Marat* (1793), *Napoleon Crossing the Saint-Bernard* (1800), *The Coronation of Josephine* (1807), *Leonidas at Thermopylae* (1814) – marked successive stages in the evolution of French politics and also of

French taste. We can see in them the search for a new and heroic conception of art, which would also be closely linked to the events of the day. In these images we can trace the pre-revolutionary stirring, then the Revolution itself, the rise of Bonaparte, the transition from Consulate to Empire, and finally the Empire's fall. Only two of the paintings I have listed have classical subjects: and only one, the *Leonidas*, has figures which are largely nude. Yet the foundation is always David's conception of the male figure.

Only two 'academies' by David are known. They are paintings done when he was studying in Rome as a young man, and both are presented as figures from the Iliad – *Patroclus* and *Hector* respectively. Preparatory drawings of the nude for his mature compositions exist, but these are rather slight. However David's advocacy of a training based chiefly on drawing and painting from the nude figure, and specifically from the nude male, had the force of law for his pupils, over whom he exercised a compelling influence. They, in turn, passed on the same system to those whom they instructed.

There was a similar return to a rigorous study of the nude throughout Europe. We find the same methods of teaching in use in Germany, in Italy and in England. The French system was based on the curriculum elaborated at the Ecole des Beaux-Arts, the official forum of artistic instruction. Pupils admitted there worked towards the great competition for the Prix de Rome, which would enable those who succeeded in carrying off the prize to study for a further period at the Académie de France in Rome. The final test was a full-scale composition, on a classical or biblical theme. But before this, pupils drew the nude assiduously, and also painted the figure full-length and made half-length torso studies and *têtes d'expression* – studies of facial expression. In addition there were in Paris private ateliers, headed by celebrated painters, in which pupils could prepare for entry to the Ecole. And finally, there were 'free' schools, like the Académie Suisse – free in the sense that a model but no instruction was provided.

Similar gradations existed in England, though here the hierarchy was less defined. The Royal Academy Schools occupied a position analogous to the Ecole des Beaux-Arts in Paris. But there were also the South Kensington Schools (the predecessor of the present Royal College of Art); the Slade school, attached to London University; and private ventures such as Heatherly's School and the school run by Sir Hubert von Herkomer at Bushey. Additionally, there were highly reputable schools outside of London, such as the Glasgow School of Art. Drawing from the life played a part in all their curricula, though the insistence on it was less rigorous in some of the private academies.

The Ecole des Beaux-Arts in Paris has a fine archive of material based on the various Prix de Rome competitions held from 1797 onwards, and various subsidiary competitions held within the school. It is fascinating to compare this material with what the painters produced after they graduated, and became independent artists trying to earn a living in the market-place. The actual Prix de Rome paintings are, of course, extremely arificial – exercises in a style of 'history painting' which had already become irrelevant to contemporary concerns. The actual life studies are often striking because of their directness, and honesty of observation.

Drawing from the life, and painting from it, were essentially exercises in learning how to see. What sometimes came into conflict with this was the 'classical ideal', rooted in the aesthetic ideas of the High Renaissance; reinforced by the artists of the Bolognese Academy; and reinforced yet again by David, the founder of French neo-classicism. Characteristically, pupils in the various official academies described above were only allowed to begin drawing from life when they had shown they were competent in drawing from the antique. Their earliest models were not living men, but plaster casts of classical statues. Knowledge of this situation has led historians of academic art to assert that the life studies produced during the 19th century were fundamentally classical in style. Even a cursory examination of the material will soon show that this statement needs to be heavily qualified, and perhaps in many cases discarded altogether.

First one needs to consider not merely the artists themselves, but what, and specifically whom, they drew and painted. It is sometimes asserted that the art schools had to rely on old derelicts, whom their unfortunate pupils struggled to idealise. The visual evidence, and indeed inscriptions preserved on some of the drawings, demonstrate the untruth of this. A sheet by William Calderon, later famous as a painter of animals, notes that the model was 'Mr Anderson, the miner'. One by Sir George Hayter is inscribed 'William Bewlay, Police Sergeant, aged 26'. Handsome well-built working-class men appeared to have been happy to pose

**Italian School** early 19th century
Standing Man seen from the rear
black, red and white chalks on paper  (51 x 35)cm
an associated label reads 'ACCADEMIA DI GALIARDI IL VECCHIA'

This Italian Academy is typical of the classical style of drawing being taught in Rome during the first half of the 19th century. The schools in Rome were the leading influence for artists from all over Europe at this period.

in the nude for a small fee. Many of the models seem to have been off-duty soldiers; others were young Italians, who made modelling their profession, both in Paris and in London.

There seems to have been no awkwardness among the models about total nudity, despite the notorious prudishness of 19th-century society, especially in England. The reason was that art schools remained sexually segregated. Women began to make an appearance as students in life-classes only comparatively late in the century. When they did appear, trouble began. The most notorious incident occurred not in England, but in the United States. Thomas Eakins (1844-1916), the greatest realist painter America has ever produced, and director of the school at the Pennsylvania Academy of the Fine Arts, put great emphasis on drawing and painting from the nude. He insisted that the model, whether male or female, must necessarily be completely unclad. 'To describe and show an important muscle as arising from some exact origin to insert itself in some indefinite manner under the breach clout is so trifling and undignified that I shall never attempt it,' he wrote to the Art Students' League of New York, who had invited him to teach.

The trouble was that, by the early 1880s, about half the students in the Pennsylvania Academy of Fine Arts were women. Even if these did not object to the traditional nudity of the life-class, then their mothers did. In 1882, one of these mothers wrote an impassioned letter to James L. Claghorn, President of the Academy. It ran in part:

> Now, Mr. Claghorn, does this pay? Does it pay for a young lady of refined godly household to be urged as the only way of obtaining a knowledge of true Art, to enter a class where every feeling of *maidenly* delicacy is violated, where she becomes so hardened to indelicate sights and words... that *no possible* art can restore her lost treasure of *chaste and delicate thoughts*.

A long struggle followed – one which it was impossible for Eakins to win. Early in 1876, the Academy asked for his resignation.

The influx of women into the traditional art schools, which probably took place somewhat earlier in the United States than it did in Europe, weakened the hitherto unchallenged authority of the life-class, by introducing sexual overtones which had hitherto been absent. The downfall of the established academic curriculum was completed by the rise of modernism, and by the 1920s the life-class was already in decay, openly scorned by students, and even instructors, who espoused progressive tendencies.

It would be a mistake, however, to conclude from this brief account that life drawing and life painting remained static throughout their 19th century heyday. The images produced underwent a subtle process of change, in response to changes in the cultural climate of the time. In general, the life drawings of the earlier years of the century are more impersonal, less portrait-like, than they become later. The bodies are more apt to be idealised, and the heads are often, though not always, more impersonal. The movement towards realism – towards the specific – is reflected in life-drawing and painting just as it is in other categories of art. At the same time artists increasingly shy away from any hint of the heroic or transcendental – there are often hints of these qualities in life drawings by early 19th-century artists such as George Hayter (1792-1871). The later works are closer to being portraits – very complete and telling portraits because they record, not merely the sitter's features, but all his physical idiosyncracies.

Because of the circumstances in which they were made, with no need to flatter the subject, or even to take his own feelings about himself into consideration, these likenesses often have unique directness. This is the case, for example, with the two torso studies by John Henry Lorimer (1856-1936) included in this book. These were evidently painted in the studio of Emile Auguste Carolus-Duran (1838-1917), with whom Lorimer studied in Paris. They show clear evidence of Carolus-Duran's admiration for Velasquez, and his insistence that his pupils study Velasquez's work. What Lorimer has taken from the great Spanish master in this instance is not his loose free handling, but his absolute objectivity. As a result the paintings are extraordinarily specific – more specific than anything Lorimer produced in his later career as a successful portraitist – and also full of character and atmosphere.

The two pictures I have just mentioned were undoubtedly produced as student exercises, though Lorimer was already in his late twenties when they were done. It is, however, a mistake to think of 19th-century academic portrayals of the male nude as being always and essentially prentice work. Some are unquestionably the work of students. The superb drawing by the future Pre-Raphaelite John Everett Millais (1829-1896) was produced when the artist was only seventeen, and bears out the legend of Millais' precociousness. The William Calderon drawing was done when the artist was only fifteen. However, some artists continued to make academic studies of the nude throughout their working lives. A case in point is William Etty (1787-1849). A large part of Etty's surviving output consists of painted studies of this kind. Other artists, already mature, drew the nude as a maeans of instructing others. The very accomplished academic drawings of Adolphe Valette (1876-1942) all seems to date from the first two decades of the century, when he was teaching drawing in Manchester.

One of the most interesting of the 'mature' nudes, not least for its ambitious scale – it is mature in terms of when it was produced, though not in subject matter – is the recently rediscovered *Repentant Boy* by Franz von Lenbach (1836-1904). Lenbach is now best remembered as a grandee of German official culture in the second half of the 19th century. His portraits of Wagner, Liszt, and especially his likenesses of Bismark, who became a close friend, were his claim to fame amongst his contemporaries. But Lenbach was a more various artist than this might lead one to suppose. In the 1850s he painted realistic landscapes and images of children which show the influence of Courbet. At the end of his life he produced a small group of paintings of the nude. The best known is the voluptuous *Madame Feez*, reclining on a couch, which is now in the Städtisches Galerie im Lenbachhaus in Munich. This is signed and dated 1902. The present picture is unsigned, but is precisely comparable in technique, and must belong to the same epoch. When the nude of Madame Feez was shown in Paris in 1984-5, in the survey exhibition *Symboles at Realités: la peinture allemande 1848-1905*, the catalogue remarked that it was 'l'un des derniers fleurons de la grande peinture traditionelle du salon'. The same comment seems appropriate here. One curious detail, however, is the presence of the triangular wooden block under the sole of the boy's right foot. Such blocks were used, as were ropes and other devices, to help the model keep the pose. Its inclusion, in what would otherwise be an atmospheric study of mood – the present title is authentic, and comes from an old label on the back of the painting – is a tribute, the more telling for being quite evidently unconscious, to Lenbach's origins as a doctrinaire socialist.

The present collection of images, though it includes some major names, only skims the surface of an immense subject. It is, however, the first anthology of academic male nudes of this period to be published, at least to my knowledge, and as such will, I think, be of great interest, not only to collectors, who are gradually discovering the fascinations of this unexplored terrain; but to practising artists, many of whom are returning to the life-class as a means of refining their technical skills, and recovering part of the heritage which was submerged by the irresistable tide of modernism.

Edward Lucie-Smith
London 1988.

**William Etty** RA  1787-1849
Rear view of a Male Nude
oil on board  (46 x 26)cm

William Etty was born in York and demonstrated his love of art from an early age. He entered the Royal Academy Schools
in 1807 and in 1808 studied under Lawrence.
Etty constantly attracted controversy by his determination to paint the nude figure. A review in 'The Times' of 1822 stated
'Nakedness without purity is offensive and indecent, and in Mr. Etty's canvass is mere dirty flesh'. But Etty was persistent
in his determinatioin to paint the nude even if it was 'unfashionable' and spent some time every day at the life classes at the
Royal Academy.

*above*

**Richard Rothwell** RHA 1800-1868

Seated Figure in profile

charcoal with white highlighting (36 x 52)cm

Rothwell was born in Athlone, Ireland and after training in Dublin became Sir Thomas Lawrence's chief assistant for many years. This study was executed in Rome circa 1835, after Lawrence's death, but the kinship to the latter's style is apparent. Rome was the main inspiration for artists from all over Europe at the beginning of the 19th century. For the unmarried bachelor such as Rothwell there was the added advantage of escaping from the restraints of British society.

*opposite*

**Eyre Crowe** 1824-1910

Half-length Figure holding a staff

pencil and coloured crayon (40 x 27)cm
signed and dated August 5th 1846

Crowe was a pupil of Paul Delaroche, with whom he went to Rome in 1843, and a life-long friend of Gerome. He travelled to America as secretary to his cousin, Thackeray, in 1852 which provided the inspiration for his most famous painting, 'The Sale of Slaves at Richmond, Virginia'. He exhibited at the Royal Academy from 1846, and became ARA in 1875.

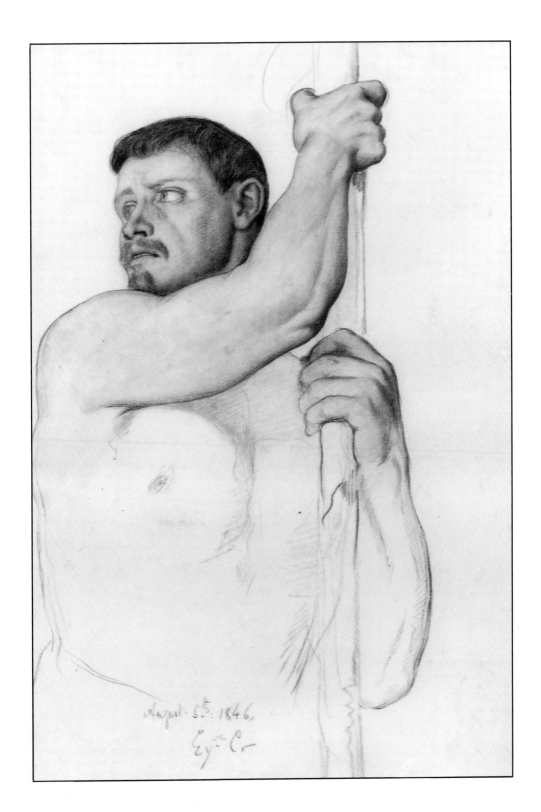

August 5ᵗʰ 1846,
Eyᵗ C

**Sir George Hayter** 1792-1871
William Bewlay, Police Sergeant, aged 26

pencil on paper (46 x 31)cm
inscribed and dated March 1848

A study for his painting 'The Angels Ministering unto Christ'. It is hard to imagine today a policeman modelling in the nude in his spare time to supplement his income.

**Abraham Cooper** RA 1787-1868
Mr. MacDowell

pencil on paper (34 x 23)cm
initialed, inscribed and dated May 1856

At the age of thirteen Cooper joined a circus where he started to draw and paint horses. Largely self-taught he became the pre-eminent British painter of battle scenes in the 19th century. This drawing of one of his visitors is typical of his use of friends as models and of the technique that artists used of drawing the figures in the nude to create the correct anatomical articulation. Only after the preliminary drawing would the artist 'clothe' his figure.

*above*

**Alfred Edward Chalon** RA 1780-1860

Figure in repose

chalks on grey paper (21 x 36)cm
signed with monogram and dated 1844

Chalon was the first artist to paint Queen Victoria on her accession to the throne and was appointed Portrait Painter to HM the Queen.

*opposite*

**Sir John Everett Millais** Bt PRA HRI HRCA 1829-1896

Standing Figure with Staff

pencil on paper (56 x 37)cm
signed with monogram and dated 1846

Although only 17 when this drawing was executed Millais was already a proficient and respected artist. He had entered the RA Schools in 1840 and exhibited his first painting at the Royal Academy in 1846. It was only two years later that with Holman Hunt and D. G. Rossetti he founded the Pre-Raphaelite Brotherhood. Of his later paintings 'Bubbles' was given the greatest publicity, being used by Pear's Soap for their advertisements.

**Alfred Elmore** RA 1815-1891

*above –* Figure leaning back with a mirror image in outline
charcoal with white highlights (4 5 x 29)cm

*opposite –* Striding Figure seen from the rear
coloured crayons on paper (44 x 28)cm

After learning to draw from the sculptures in the British Museum, Elmore studied at the Royal Academy Schools from 1832. He then travelled to Paris, Munich and Rome before returning to London in 1842 and exhibited at the Royal Academy regularly until his death.

**William Edward Frost** RA 1810-1877
Man Standing with Sword
pen and wash with watercolour (12 x 8)cm

A late neo-classicist, Frost was an early protege of Etty, and there is a reflection of Etty's style in his work generally.

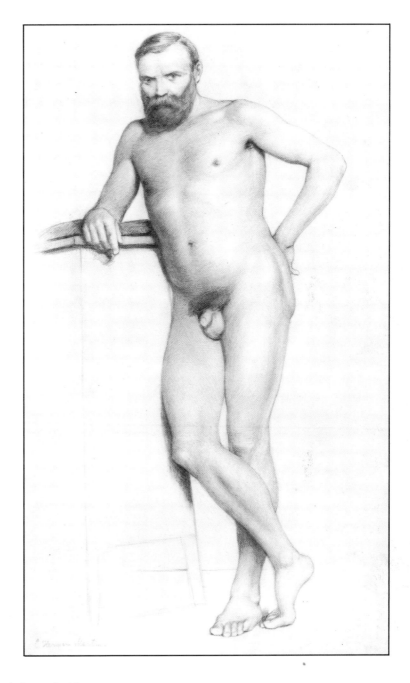

**Carl Hermann Martini** 1796-1869
Standing Figure – full frontal
pencil on paper (44 x 26)cm signed

Martini lived and worked in Biberach whose museum shows his work which is mainly of animal subjects. Martini belonged to the generation of the Nazarenes and this drawing, with its near-photographic realistic approach, clearly shows their influence.

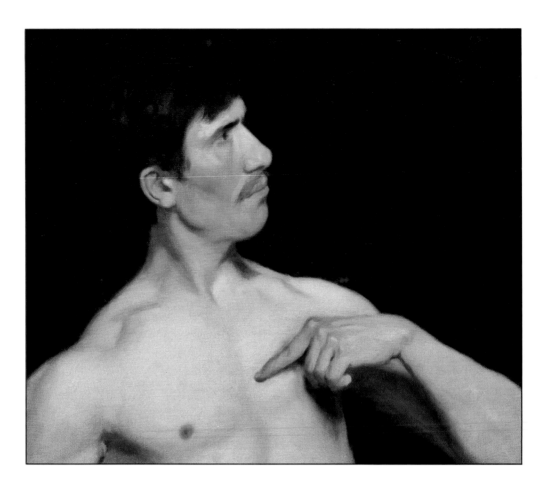

**John Henry Lorimer** RSA RSW RWS    1856-1936
*above* – A Head and Shoulders in Profile
oil on canvas  (53 x 64)cm

*opposite* – Study of a Head and Torso
oil on canvas  (72 x 58)cm

Born in Edinburgh, Lorimer first studied at the RSA under McTaggart and later in Paris under Carolus Duran, 1884. He exhibited at the RSA from 1873 and at the RA from 1878. In his early years he concentrated on portraiture and flower painting but was later to win distinction as a painter of contemporary genre. His work was popular in France and came to be associated with the members of the Glasgow School of whom the leaders were Sir James Guthrie and Sir John Lavery.

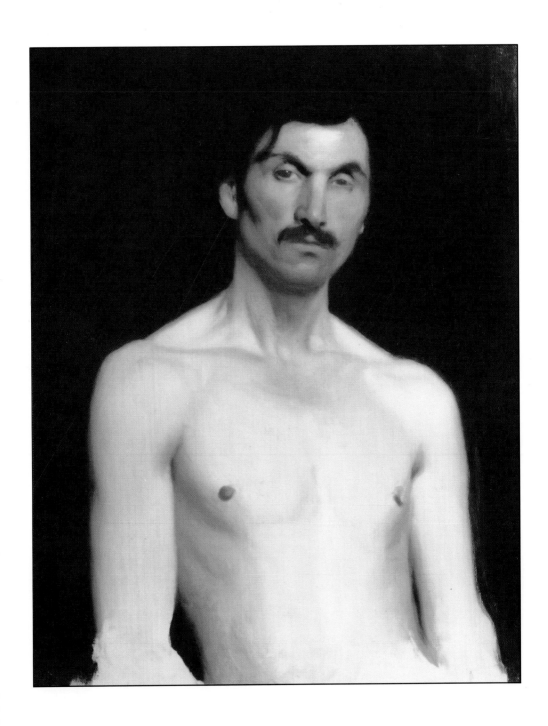

*page 35*
**South Kensington School**   circa 1860-80
Male Nude Study
oil on paper  (28 x 15)cm


*page 36*
**George Fiddes Watt** RSA RP  1873-1960
Standing Figure
oil on canvas

One of several Scottish artists featured in this collection, Fiddes Watt specialised in portrait painting. This canvas dates from around 1890.


*page 37*
**Pierre-Paul Boissart**   exhibiting 1911-1938
member of La Société des Artistes Franøais
A Model at a Life Class
oil on canvas  (161 x 65)cm

From the dress of the artist shown at the right-hand bottom corner this lively canvas was painted around 1910. The style has links to Bonnard. Later paintings by the same artist resemble work by members of the Newlyn group in England.


*page 38*
**David Ghilchik** ROI  b.1892
Standing Figure, full face with a vase of flowers
oil on canvas  (92 x 61)cm

Born in Romania, Ghilchik studied at Manchester and at the Slade School under Tonks and McEvoy. He exhibited at the Royal Academy and elsewhere but was also well-known as an illustrator and as a contributor to 'Punch' between 1920 and 1939. This fine painting dates from around 1920.

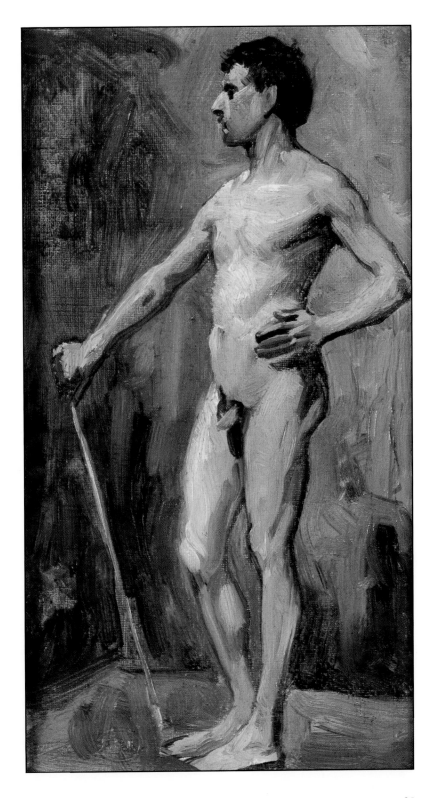

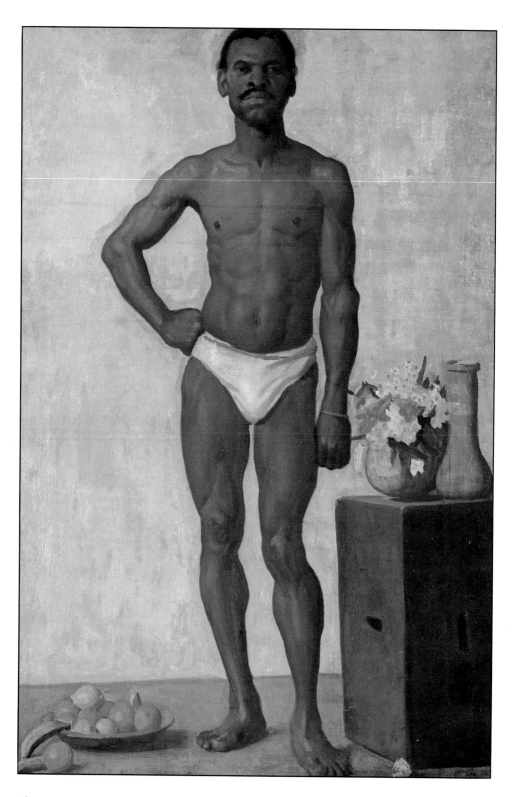

**Alphonse Legros** RE 1837-1911

Standing Figure with staff. With rework of head at base.

charcoal on paper (51 x 28)cm

Although being French, Legros was to be a major influence in English Academic drawing in the latter half of the 19th century. Encouraged by Whistler he came to England in 1863 and within a few years was appointed teacher of etching at the South Kensington School of Art, whose pupils contribute to the exhibition. Afterwards he was to move to the Slade as Professor of Fine Art from 1876 to 1892. Among the many pupils he influenced was the young William Calderon, one of whose studies is featured here. He also may have influenced Sir Hubert von Herkomer who entered South Kensington in 1866. Herkomer was to found his own school at Bushey and his most famous pupil, Lucy Kemp-Welch, whose work is also represented in this collection, was to take over the school and continue the academic tradition.

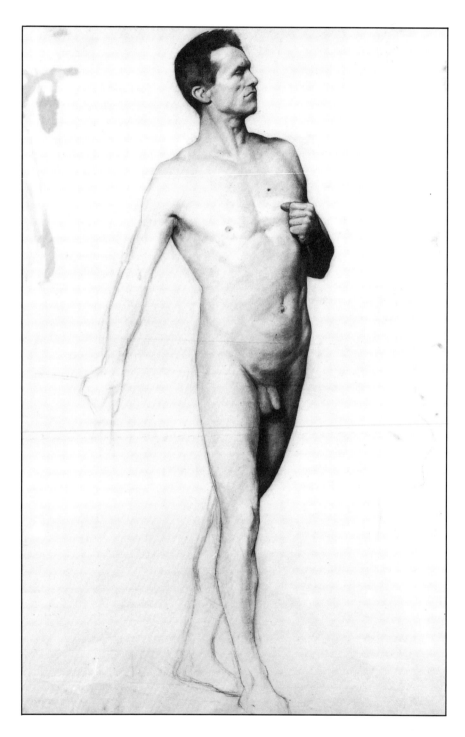

**French School** mid-19th century
Standing Figure Facing Right, left-hand raised to the chest
charcoal on laid paper (64 x 48)cm

**40**

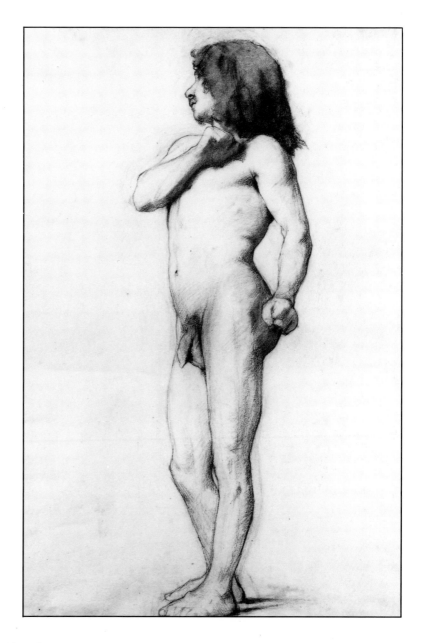

**French School** mid-19th century
Standing Figure facing left, right hand raised to chest
charcoal on laid paper (62 x 49)cm

The two studies here are typical of the work being produced by leading students at the Paris Ecole des Beaux-Arts at this period. The classicism instilled by Jacques-Louis David and his successors was being transformed by a new current of realism, and the drawings have a strangely portrait-like quality which is irrelevant to their main purpose as academic studies.

**Lucy Elizabeth Kemp-Welch** RI 1869-1958
Figure Seated on stool
charcoal on paper (56 x 32)cm

Lucy Kemp-Welch studied under Herkomer at Bushey from 1891 and took over the school in 1905 until 1926. Exhibited at the Royal Academy from 1894 mainly with animal subjects and particularly horses.

**William Frank Calderon** ROI 1865-1943

Rear view of a standing Man holding a staff above his head

charcoal highlighted with white on green paper (4 5 x27)cm

inscribed 'W. Anderson, the Miner, March 1880'

Calderon was a pupil of Legros at the Slade and although this drawing may seem mature for a fifteen-year-old, he was to exhibit his first picture at the Royal Academy the very next year – 1881. His main reputation was as an animal painter.

**Sir Edward John Poynter** PRA, RWS 1836-1919

Study of a Classical Youth, possibly Mercury, with subsidiary studies

charcoal with white highlights on buff paper (37 x 31)cm

Poynter was renowned as an academic artist and these studies would certainly be done from life. He made many preparatory drawings for every figure in his paintings and also worked on book illustrations, stained glass windows, medals, tiles and murals. Like his contemporary, Alma-Tadema, he favoured Greek and Roman subjects, mostly figures in marble interiors. He was President of the Royal Academy from 1896 to 1918.

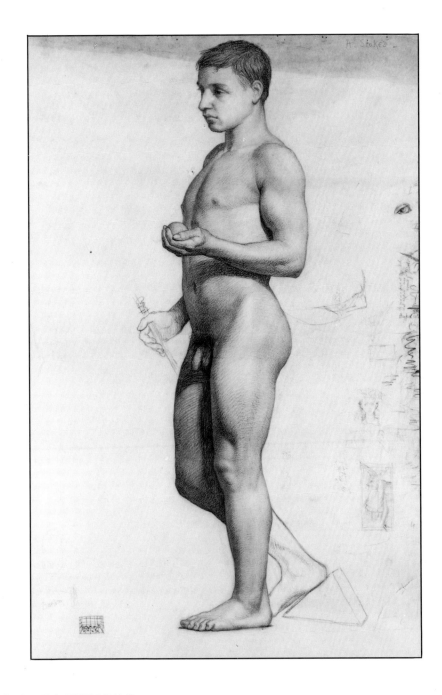

**Adrian Scott Stokes** RA RWS NEAC 1854-1935

Standing Figure

pencil on paper   (71 x 4 5)cm

After training in London and Paris, Stokes travelled widely in Europe, painting land and seascapes which he particularly enjoyed doing in the open air.

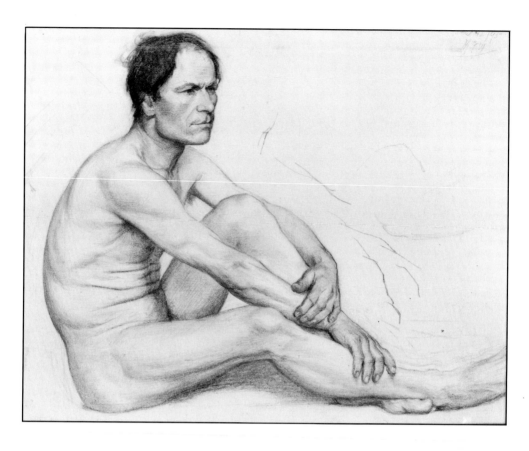

**Duncan MacGregor Whyte** 1866-1953

*above* – Seated Figure

black chalk on paper (48 x 62)cm
initialled and dated Jan 12 95

*opposite* – Seated Figure in Profile

charcoal on paper (61 x 46)cm

Macgregor Whyte studied in Glasgow, Paris and Antwerp and exhibited at the RSA and GI. He also lived and worked for many years in Australia. The models for these powerful drawings were quite possibly soldiers, many of whom used to sit for artists to earn extra money. They were excellent subjects, not only because of their fine physique, but as they were trained to stand still for sustained periods.

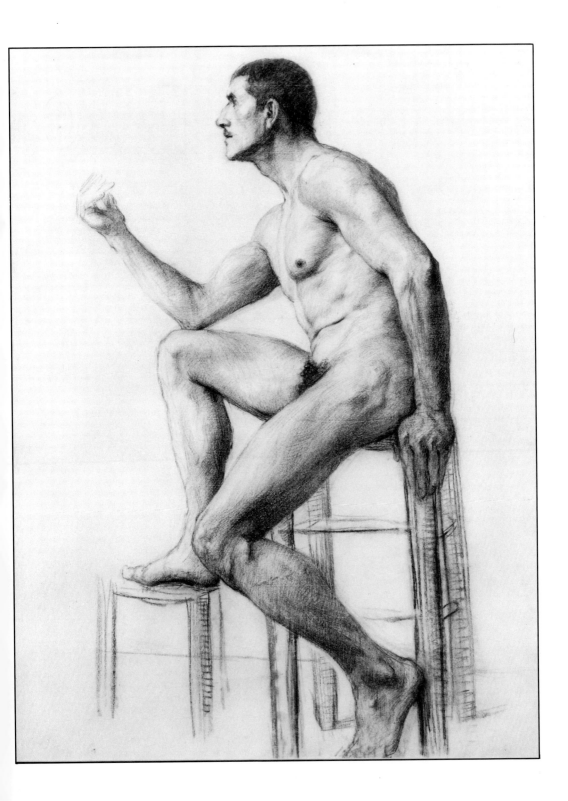

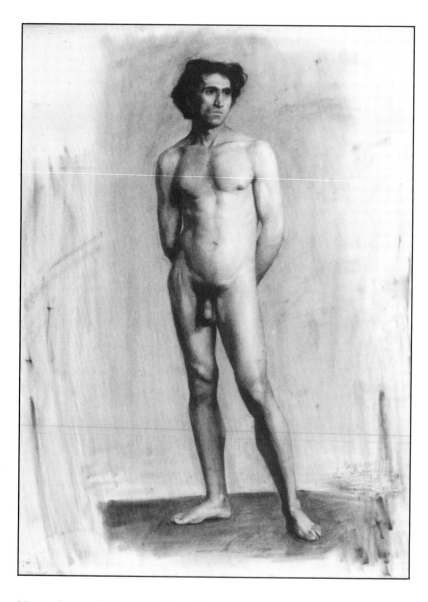

**Henry James Haley** – studying 1897-99

*above* – Figure Standing with hands behind his back

charcoal on paper (76 x 56)cm
inscribed 'Oct 29 1898  J. S. Sargent'

*opposite* – Standing Full Frontal – left hand raised to face

charcoal and wash on laid paper (75 x 53)cm
inscribed 'Feb 27 1897  Marcus Stone'

These two fine studies are from a set of life drawings executed for a competition at the Royal Academy Schools and illustrate well the high standard of drawing achieved at this period. They are inscribed with the name of the tutor. Haley afterwards exhibited paintings of interiors at the Royal Academy and was also known as a silversmith.

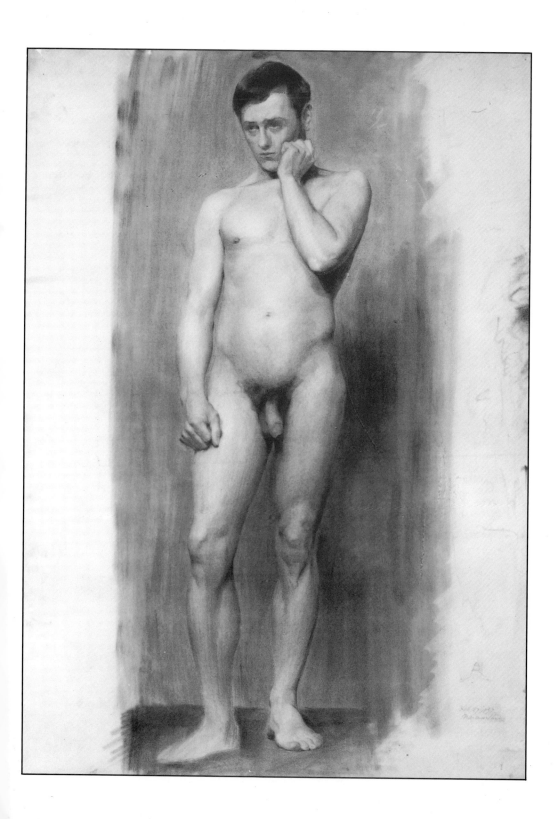

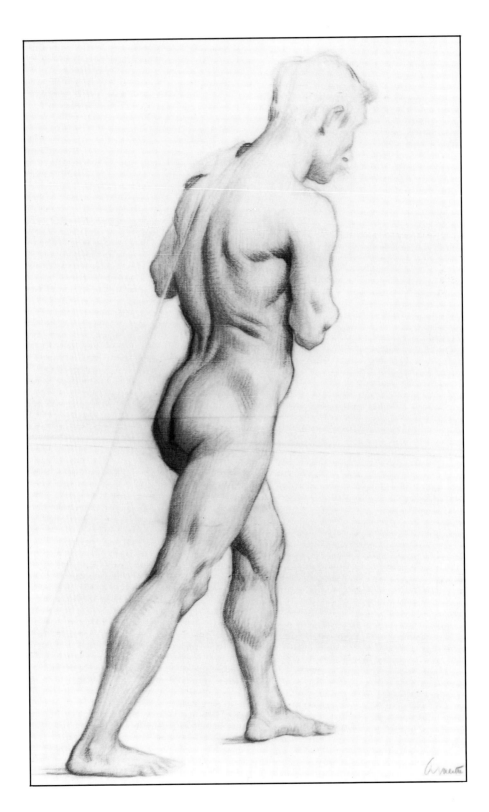

**Adolphe Valette  1876-1942**

*above* – Man Pulling on Rope

pencil and red crayon on paper  (60 x 37)cm
signed

*opposite* – Man Bending Over

red crayon on paper  (34 x 26)cm
initialled

Born in Saint-Etienne, France, Valette moved to Manchester in 1904, where he was a celebrated teacher of life drawing. His best remembered pupil was L. S. Lowry, who was greatly influenced by him and who remained grateful to Valette's teaching throughout his life. These drawings, dating from around 1905, are masterly studies in the style of Tonks.

**Harold Speed** RSPP 1872-1957

*above* – Full Reclining Figure from the Rear
red chalk on laid paper (4 5 x 58)cm

*opposite* – Three-quarter-length Reclining Figure
red chalk on orange paper highlighted in white (50 x 35)cm

Speed studied at the RA Schools 1891-96 and exhibited at the Royal Academy from 1893. His early works were inspired by the high Victorian classical painters and he later turned to portrait painting. These two drawings executed around 1910-20 clearly show a fresh sensitive and sensual approach to the male figure.

**Henry Holiday** 1839-1927
Running Man

pencil on brown paper (50 x 33)cm

Holiday started his artistic training at the early age of 13 and entered the Royal Academy Schools in 1855. He was immediately drawn towards the Pre-Raphaelite movement and soon became associated with its leading members. In 1862 he succeeded Burne-Jones at the Whitefriars Glass Works, designing stained glass windows, and this was to become his major work for the rest of his life.

**Keith Henderson** RWS RSW ROI  1883-1955
A Youth Rising Up from Under Water

pencil on paper  (57 x 46)cm

Henderson studied at the Slade School and in Paris. He both illustrated and wrote several books including 'Prehistoric Man'. His paintings are represented in many public collections.

**Herbert Davis Richter** RI RSW ROI  1874-1955
Study of a Boy lying on his back

pencil on paper  (20 x 25)cm

Richter studied at Lambeth and the London School of Art under Brangwyn and J. M. Swan, exhibiting at the Royal Academy from 1906. This study is from a sketchbook with many figures clothed in typical Edwardian style and must date from the period immediately preceding the First World War. Perhaps surprisingly Richter is not known for figures but for flowers. He published 'Flower Painting in Oil and Watercolour' and many other works.

*List of abbreviations*

RA     Royal Academy
RHA    Royal Hibernian Academy
ARA    Associate of RA
PRA    President of RA
H      Honorary member of ...
RE     Royal Society of Painter-Etchers & Engravers
RI     Royal Institute of Painters in Watercolours
ROI    Royal Institute of Oil Painters
RWS    Royal Society of Painters in Watercolours
RP
RSPP   Royal Society of Portrait Painters
RSA    Royal Scottish Academy of Painting, Sculpture and
       Architecture
GI     Royal Glasgow Institute for Fine Art Society
RSW    Royal Scottish Society of Painters in Watercolours
NEAC   New English Art Club

ART from

THE GAY MEN'S PRESS

Philip Core
PAINTINGS: 1975-1985
Introduced by George Melly
Philip Core is an American painter resident in London and his much-
celebrated paintings are informed by strong gay cultural themes.
40 colour plates
(200 x 200)mm, 96 pages, £9.95 hardback

Mario Dubsky
TOM PILGRIM'S PROGRESS AMONG THE CONSEQUENCES OF
CHRISTIANITY
Introduced by Edward Lucie-Smith
Mario Dubsky was struck down at the height of his artistic career by the
deadly AIDS virus. This collection of his pencil drawings stands as a
testament to his position as a powerful gay artist.
64 black & white plates
(240 x 225)mm, 84 pages, £4.95 paperback

Juan Davila
HYSTERICAL TEARS
Edited by Paul Taylor
Juan Davila is a gay Chilean artist now living and working in Australia. His
paintings constantly knock the Western world's artistic establishment from a
unique combination of third-world and gay consciousness. His work has won
international fame and notoriety and utterly shocked the Australian authorities.
35 colour plates
(200 x 200)mm, 108 pages, £7.95 paperback, £14.95 hardback

Roberto González Fernandez
JOURNEYS
Introduced by John Russell Taylor
González is one of Spain's leading modern painters. In his super-photorealistic
style which is both erotic and informative he portrays the world of late
20th-century gay man — a world not only preoccupied with itself but with the
myriad problems facing thinking humanity.
39 colour plates, 11 black & white plates
(228 x 254)mm, 60 pages, £14.95 paperback

Duncan Grant
PRIVATE: The Erotic Art of Duncan Grant
Introduced by Douglas Blair Turnbaugh
This is the book of Douglas Blair Turnbaugh s unique collection of Duncan
Grant s homoerotic work bequeathed to him on the understanding that it
would be published. Light, airy, humorous and very amorous these drawings
and paintings will both delight and charm.
37 colour plates, 22 black & white
(228 x 254)mm, 80 pages, £25.00 hardback

David Hutter
**NUDES AND FLOWERS**
**Introduced by Edward Lucie-Smith**
David Hutter is a master English watercolourist. This exquisite collection of
delicate watercolours is primarily of the modern male nude combined with a
series of tender flower paintings.
40 colour plates
(200 x 200)mm, 96 pages, £9.50 paperback

Michael Leonard
**CHANGING**
**Introduced by Edward Lucie-Smith**
These highly-charged pencil drawings of males undressing have become a
universal classic.
50 black & white plates
(200 x 200)mm, 112 pages, £7.95 paperback

Michael Leonard
**PAINTINGS**
**The Artist in conversation with Edward Lucie-Smith**
This is a comprehensive collection of Michael Leonard's paintings executed
from the early 1970s to the present day in the widely popular photorealist
style. Subject matter ranges from portraiture and townscapes to the male
nude.
40 colour plates
(200 x 200)mm, 104 pages, £14.95 hardback

Cornelius McCarthy
**INTERIORS**
**Introduced by Emmanuel Cooper**
A modern painter whose work embodies exciting form, colour and content and
informed throughout with a highly charged homoerotic sensibility.
40 colour plates
(200 x 200)mm, 64 pages, £8.95 paperback, £14.95 hardback

Peter Samuelson
**POST-WAR FRIENDS**
**Introduced by John Russell Taylor**
These paintings and drawings capture something of the style, time and place
of Britain in the period immediately following the Second World War.
10 black & white, 20 colour plates
(210 x 148)mm, 48 pages  £6.95

Douglas Simonson
**HAWAII**
Douglas Simonson's paintings and drawings focus on the beautiful Pacific
male. They are both visually stunning and quietly erotic and manage to bring
to the viewer something of the atmosphere of these beautiful Pacific islands
and their people.
40 colour plates
(200 x 200)mm, 64 pages, £8.95 paperback, £14.95 hardback

**Nick Stanley (ed.)**
**OUT IN ART**
**Christopher Brown, Chris Corr, Norman, Richard Royle, Graham Ward**
Five modern gay British artists. This widely acclaimed collection embraces
five very different visualities though all are imbued with contemporary gay
consciousness and a vibrant homoeroticism.
37 colour plates
(200 x 200)mm, 64 pages, £7.95 paperback, £14.95 hardback

**Emmanuel Cooper**
**THE LIFE AND WORK OF HENRY SCOTT TUKE**
Henry Scott Tuke (1858-1929) was known in his time as 'the painter of
youth', and indeed this beautiful monograph by one of Britain's leading gay
art critics vindicates his reputation admirably. This is the first ever collection
of his famous paintings and most plates are in full colour.
20 black & white/36 colour plates
(256 x 228)mm, 72 pages, £25 hardback

**PLEASE SEND FOR OUR COMPLETE CATALOGUE TO:**

**GMP Publishers Ltd**
**P O Box 247**
**London N17 9QR**

**And we will forward it by return.**

GMP books can be ordered from any bookshop in the UK, and from
specialised bookshops overseas.
If you prefer to order by mail, please send full retail price plus £2.00 for
postage and packing to GMP Publishers Ltd (M.O.), PO Box 247, London
N17 9QR, England. Telephone 01-365 154 5.

(For Access/Eurocard/Mastercharge/American Express give number and
signature.) Comprehensive mail-order catalogue also available.

In North America order from Alyson Publications Inc., 40 Plympton St, Boston
MA 02118, U S A.

NAME AND ADDRESS IN BLOCK LETTERS PLEASE:

Name ...........................................

Address ........................................

......................................................

......................................................

......................................................